THE MALVERN HILLS

THE MALVERN HILLS

Mike Smart

F

FRANCES LINCOLN LIMITED

PUBLISHERS

Frances Lincoln Limited
4 Torriano Mews, Torriano Avenue, London NW5 2RZ
www.franceslincoln.com

The Malvern Hills
Copyright © Frances Lincoln Limited 2009
Text and photographs © Mike Smart 2009

First Frances Lincoln edition: 2009

British Library Cataloguing in Publication data
A catalogue record for this book is available from the British Library.

ISBN: 978-0-7112-2915-0

Printed and bound in Singapore

9 8 7 6 5 4 3 2 1

HALF TITLE
Rising above the morning mist: Table Hill, Sugarloaf Hill, Worcestershire Beacon and Summer Hill viewed along the western flanks from British Camp.

TITLE PAGE
Moody and magnificent, the sun making a real effort to break through the rain clouds over Bredon Hill to the west.

ABOVE
Beauty and the beast. One of the many gentle giants to be found grazing high on the hill.

RIGHT
Below Jubilee Hill, behind these rocks, is a comfortable bench, discreetly tucked away and out of the wind, always a favourite place to stop, get out the flask and savour the view eastwards across the vale towards Bredon Hill.

CONTENTS

FOREWORD

Welcome to the Malvern Hills. Between Herefordshire and Worcestershire the Malvern Hills form a beautiful, distinctive range of peaks and gullies running south for nine miles from Great Malvern to Chase End. Towering above Great Malvern itself is Worcestershire Beacon. At 1,395 feet (485 metres) it is the highest peak in the range.

Within a relatively small area of countryside, the Malvern Hills boast a number of diverse landscapes, rich in wildlife, flora and fauna. In addition to the visitors attracted by the various walks, open spaces and dramatic vistas, the Hills are a popular destination for those interested in everything from hang gliding and moth trapping to horse riding and orienteering.

The caretakers of the Hills are the Malvern Hills Conservators, a public body established by an Act of Parliament in 1884. The Hills Conservators are charged with the following primary tasks:

- To keep the land as close to nature as possible and encourage wildlife
- To secure open space for public recreation and enjoyment
- To protect those with rights as registered commoners
- To prevent encroachment

Who has access over the Hills?

The Malvern Hills Conservators are governed by five Acts of Parliament. The first Act of 1884 enshrines the right of access on foot and historically on horseback to all the common land under the Hills Conservators' jurisdiction. This is supplemented by the right-of-way network that superimposes footpaths and bridleways over the land, hence the added right for cyclists to use bridleways.

Looking north from North Hill, each dip in the rolling countryside is identified by its very own cloud.

Three full-time wardens and voluntary wardens patrol the area to oversee the byelaws and help visitors with their enquiries.

A warm welcome

Man's best friend is always welcome as hills are a wonderful place for dog walkers. All we ask is your owners be 'considerate' and clear-up what you leave behind.

Mountain bikers are also welcome to experience the hills and are requested to keep to the bridleways (marked on OS maps) and ride in a courteous and considerate manner.

Challenges

There will always be challenges to face, and they are always easier to overcome with the support of, and in partnership with, our guests. So we extend a warm welcome to all the visitors to our Hills and Commons; please make the most of this wonderful place and enjoy your precious leisure time.

Our future

The management of the Hills is a balancing act between acting in the interests of visitors and conserving this ancient landscape and its wildlife. Whether or not we are succeeding is for you to judge. Please help us by giving us feedback about your experience or concerns. There are many competing factors in managing this unique area, it is not always possible for us to act on every request; but we will always do our best.

Malvern Hills Conservators
Manor House
Malvern
Worcestershire, WR14 3EY
01684 892002
www.malvernhills.org.uk

INTRODUCTION

The Malvern Hills landscape has fired the imagination of painters, poets, writers, composers and scientists for many years. And it's not lost any of its power to surprise, charm and thrill.

In this, my collection of images of the Malvern Hills, I have attempted to capture what I feel is the 'Spirit of the Hills'. You will soon discover the pictures in this book do not appear in order of geographic position or by season or by size of hill. This is a rambling, meandering collection and, just like a wander on the hills, reveals a new and unexpected view with each turn of the page.

Geographically, the Malvern Hills run almost directly north–south along the Herefordshire–Worcestershire border, dipping into Gloucestershire at its southernmost end. The special quality of the Malverns lies in its contrasts. It is an easily identifiable narrow ridge that thrust above the patchwork farmland of the Severn Vale 600 million years ago, producing a mountain range in miniature.

A journey along the rhythmic sawtooth Malvern ridge is a voyage of discovery. Each hill possesses its own distinctive character.

Starting in the north, the first hill we encounter is shy End Hill (1,079ft), small in comparison to its brothers, but don't be fooled. The path from the North Malvern Road through the trees is steep and taxing, especially when wet. However, the rewarding views to the north and west are soon evident. The upward trudge is deceptive: you think you have reached the peak four times only to find more climbing awaits. Fortunately, each ramp is less steep than the last. Once on the top of End Hill the splendour of North and Table Hills, with their adjoining saddle, is revealed.

It is here too that you are treated to your first view of Shire Ditch. The Ditch runs up the valley to the east and over the saddle before you. It is believed that Shire Ditch earthwork was built by Gilbert de Clare, the Red Earl of Gloucester, in about 1287, during a boundary dispute with the Bishop of Hereford. The Red Earl married the daughter of Edward I, Joan d'Arce, and in doing so received the hunting rights to Malvern Chase. The Ditch will accompany us on our voyage all the way to Hollybush some seven miles or so to the south.

A quick descent followed by a short, sharp, grassy climb delivers you to the east–west Lady Howard de Walden Path. This well contoured path is worn like a belt around the waist of these two hills and provides level walking with spectacular views over the town. The path is wide, built purposely for three horsemen to ride side by side when hunting.

Rounded Table Hill (1,224ft), with an even covering of deep strength-sapping grass, is a haven for skylarks and radio-controlled model aircraft flyers. Its slopes fall away evenly on the west into its wooded skirt and West Malvern.

Its nearest neighbour, across the saddle to the east, is arrogant North Hill (1,303ft), where, following a stiff march, you'll discovery a rocky bare peak, almost barren of vegetation. This hill stands strong and stubborn against the weather that comes from the north, protecting its companions. On its steep slopes rocky outcrops are clearly visible, protruding through the vegetation like bony elbows through worn woollen sleeves. The path to the south is comfortable enough, dropping down towards Green Valley and offering stunning views of Worcestershire Beacon. Paths to the north, however, are different, starting on a gradual slope and getting steeper and

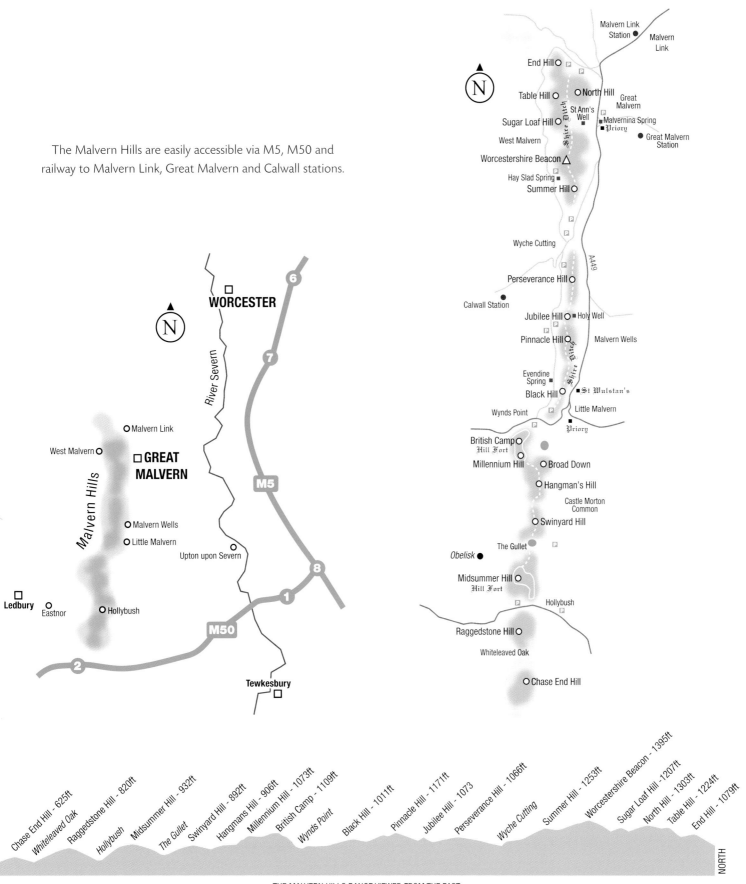

The Malvern Hills are easily accessible via M5, M50 and railway to Malvern Link, Great Malvern and Calwall stations.

N

Malvern Link Station ●
Malvern Link

End Hill ○

Table Hill ○   ● North Hill
                    St Ann's Well
                    Great Malvern
Sugar Loaf Hill ○   ■ Malvernina Spring
West Malvern   Priory
                    ● Great Malvern Station
Worcestershire Beacon △

Hay Slad Spring ■
Summer Hill ○

Shire Ditch
A449

Wyche Cutting

Perseverance Hill ○

Calwall Station ●

Jubilee Hill ○ ■ Holy Well

Pinnacle Hill ○   Malvern Wells

Evendine Spring ■
                Shire Ditch
Black Hill ○ ■ St Wulstan's
Wynds Point   Little Malvern
                   Priory
British Camp ○
Hill Fort
Millennium Hill ○   ○ Broad Down
                ○ Hangman's Hill
                Castle Morton Common
            ○ Swinyard Hill
The Gullet ○
Obelisk ●
Midsummer Hill ○
Hill Fort
                Hollybush
Raggedstone Hill ○
Whiteleaved Oak
            ○ Chase End Hill

WORCESTER

River Severn

6

N

7

Malvern Link ○

West Malvern ○   GREAT MALVERN

Malvern Hills

Malvern Wells ○
Little Malvern ○
Upton upon Severn ○

M5

Ledbury ○ Eastnor

Hollybush ○

8

1

M50

2

Tewkesbury

SOUTH

Chase End Hill - 625ft
Whiteleaved Oak
Raggedstone Hill - 820ft
Hollybush
Midsummer Hill - 932ft
The Gullet
Swinyard Hill - 892ft
Hangmans Hill - 906ft
Millennium Hill - 1073ft
British Camp - 1109ft
Wynds Point
Black Hill - 1011ft
Pinnacle Hill - 1171ft
Jubilee Hill - 1073
Perseverance Hill - 1066ft
Wyche Cutting
Summer Hill - 1253ft
Worcestershire Beacon - 1395ft
Sugar Loaf Hill -1207ft
North Hill - 1303ft
Table Hill - 1224ft
End Hill - 1079ft

NORTH

THE MALVERN HILLS RANGE VIEWED FROM THE EAST

This wonderful character stands guard outside Hollybush Manor.

Fungi on Table Hill.

steeper, not advisable when the grass is wet. After many years of quarrying on its northern slopes, which fortunately ceased in the 1950s, the deep scars have now become overgrown with vegetation and are a haven for wildlife.

Continuing south, briefly joining the Lady Howard de Walden Path, then over Hodges Way, we find elegant Sugarloaf Hill (1,207ft). Comfortable paths run around both east and west sides at varying levels, but without doubt the path over the peak offers the greatest reward: a clear view of Worcestershire Beacon and glimpses of Perseverance Hill and British Camp in the far distance.

Dropping down to meet the top end of The Dingle, we find the first of the four extremely well constructed 'cairns'. These are piles of rocks neatly held together with cement and topped off with directional arrows.

Continuing south you will be impressed by proud Worcestershire Beacon (1,395ft). Its huge bulk, the biggest of all the Malverns, dominates the southern aspect. To follow Shire Ditch (easily visible) is the quickest but hardest route to the Beacon. A much more gradual path is available. The old pony path, which glides gently from the cairn, first curves east, high above St Ann's Well, then swings west, gradually and evenly round to the Beacon's west side. The path delivers you onto the Beacon just below the trig point.

If you stand on the Beacon and look east, it is said, the next highest hills are the Urals in Russia.

Clearly visible from here is part of Malvern's Second World War history. During the war, the British government was partially evacuated to Malvern. It became the home of Telecommunications Research, renowned for its role in the history of radar.

Beacon fires have been lit on the Malverns since Norman times and it is claimed the fires can be seen from twelve counties.

The toposcope that accompanies the trig point on the Beacon top bares three inscriptions; on the north side: 'Worcestershire Beacon the highest point of the Malvern Hills 1,395ft'; on the south side: 'Erected in commemoration of the sixtieth year of Queen Victoria's Reign 1897'; and on the top around the informative map: 'The earth is the Lord's and the followers thereof'. On a clear day, the views extend south to the Bristol Channel and the Hills of Dartmoor, west to Hay Bluff and the Black Mountains, north to Titterstone Clee Hill and the Wrekin, and east to Bredon Hill and the Cotswolds Ridge. This certainly is a wonderful place to linger with your flask of tea and take in the views.

After continuing south for just a few minutes, we reach Rookery Rocks. Take a moment here before the steep, gravelly descent and wonder at the view south from this point – inspirational indeed – Summer Hill, Wyche Cutting, Perseverance Hill, Pinnacle Hill, Black Hill, Herefordshire Beacon, Midsummer Hill, the Obelisk and May Hill in the Forest of Dean are easily visible from this point.

Next is Summer Hill (1,253ft), much smaller than the previously visited hills. This is, unfortunately, as far a many visitors get when walking up from Beacon Road car park. What a shame, but it is an achievement in itself. Continuing south, the second cairn is reached, where arrows point towards the Gold Mine and Ernslaw Quarry.

Take care crossing the road at Wyche Cutting, the highest pass on the Malvern Hills. When climbing the steps, the sharp-eyed will notice the witch-shaped weather vane on top of the ornately carved bus shelter. Wyche Cutting has connections with the ancient salt way from Droitwich Spa.

On to the gradual climb of Perseverance Hill (1,066ft), here is a choice of paths on either side and straight up the middle. On the eastern side, following Shire Ditch, the path can be rough to start with because of erosion, but soon levels out to be comfortable and wide. Visible far below, on the eastern side, is the railway to Hereford passing under the hills for over a mile. Below to the west is Jubilee Drive winding its way towards the Kettle Sings Café and Herefordshire Beacon.

Continuing south and descending slightly, Jubilee Hill (1,073ft) is next on the list, small in stature and named in 2002 in commemoration of the Queen's Golden Jubilee. Just below the peak, to the west, is a rock bearing a plaque dedicated to the occasion. Near by is a grove of trees planted by the Malvern Hills Conservators in 1977 to commemorate the Queen's Silver Jubilee.

We then descend Jubilee Hill to a junction of pathways. The east path winds its way gently down through the trees, taking us past Devil's Spring and eventually to Holy Well Spring. The west path leads along the side of Pinnacle Hill and towards the Kettle Sings. Alternatively we can head south, upwards and over Pinnacle Hill.

The steady climb of Pinnacle Hill (1,171ft) is long, but worth every step. The ridge path has no trees, bushes or shrubs to hide the panoramic view. The long peak possesses two round barrows. The thermals are said to be excellent along this part of the ridge, you may see hang gliders making the best of these.

Everyone has their own particular 'best view in England', and this spot, looking south towards British Camp, just happens to be my very own.

At the bottom of the steep gravely descent, you may notice the boundary marker stones indicating the old county and

INSCRIBED
TO THE MEMORY OF
JAMES COCKS, ENSIGN IN THE GUARDS:

he was the only surviving issue of James Cocks, Esq., oldest nephew of
Lord Chancellor Somers, and of Ann, sister of the late Lord Berkeley of Stratton.
Possessed of an ample patrimony, he preferred honour to security, and before he had
attained the age of 20, fighting for his country fell in battle at St Cas on the coast
of France, A.D. 1758.

Nature provides. On the south-facing slopes of Table Hill a
solitary tree provides welcome shade.

parish boundary line. From here there is, as on all the hills, a choice of paths. Up and over the top, or the easier, alternative path around the side. Going over the top you'll discover a fence preventing you from wandering too far east; a good job too, as here on 'stubborn' Black Hill (1,011ft) quarrying has taken out almost half the hillside. To illustrate just how much stone was quarried from the hills, most of the quarries actually had their own railways built to ease the removal of quarried stone. From the top of Black Hill is an excellent view of British Camp and as we descend towards Black Hill East House and the car park, you may notice Little Malvern Priory church to the east. Now on level ground and easy walking, we swing around to the west were we find a welcoming bench. It's worth taking five minutes here to sit and take in the view of almost the whole range so far.

A steep drop delivers us to a road leading to historic British Camp, which has a car park, hotel and a small shop selling tea and coffee.

Taking great care crossing the main Malvern–Ledbury road we pass through a wooden gate, on the right there is a large stone inscribed: 'This is the British Camp of Herefordshire Beacon. One of the finest earthworks in Britain, built about the second century BC, later enlarged and altered before the Roman Conquest; it dominates the vicinity and commands magnificent panoramic views. Esteemed by John Evelyn the diarist, to be "one of the godliest vistas in England".' At a spring near by, William Langland, the famous fourteenth-century poet, 'slombred in a sleping' and dreamt his *Vision of Piers Plowman*.

A steep well-made path leads to British Camp (1,115ft). To clarify the names: this hill is Herefordshire Beacon; British Camp (one of two hill forts on the range) is the Iron Age fortress that sits upon the hill; and the top of British Camp is called the Citadel, possibly added by the Normans. The coming of the Romans ended the period of occupation of British Camp. Most visitors to the Malvern Hills will make a trip to British Camp, which is the second largest Iron Age hill fort in the country and dominates Herefordshire Beacon. The picturesque and very impressive ramparts are still clearly visible today. Originally, it was thought to have been a purely defensive facility to which people would retreat to in times of trouble. Excavations on the second hill fort on nearby Midsummer Hill, suggest that they were occupied permanently providing home for up to 4,000 people for as long as 400 or 500 years.

The Ancient Britons are probably responsible for the name Malvern, or 'moel-bryn', meaning 'the bare hill'.

Local folklore suggests that the last of the great Ancient British chieftains, Caractacus, made his last stand against the Romans on British Camp. The legend says that following his heroic battle and subsequent capture he was transported to Rome where Emperor Claudius was so impressed with accounts of his bravery that he was provided with a villa and a pension. Malvern's adopted son Sir Edward Elgar was inspired by this story to compose the cantata *Caractacus* in 1898.

British Camp offers fine views in all directions so it is easy to see why this location was chosen as a fortress. It commands views over Wynd's Point and the ridge to the north, south and Midsummer Hill. The Camp benefited from a water supply in the shape of Walm's Well, a freshwater spring. Below the Camp to the east is the reservoir and Tinkers Hill, with views across the Vale of Eversham and the Cotswolds Ridge. To the south is the Obelisk, erected to the Honourable Edward Charles Cocks. It dominates the uplands of Eastnor Deer Park and in the far distance May Hill and the Forest of Dean.

Moving south on to the lower ramparts we find ourselves on 'lumbering' Millennium Hill (1,073ft), overlooking the

British Camp rising above the trees, like a mystical beast.

ancient landscape of News Wood. Then we make our way down the zigzag path to the third cairn. From here, directly east, is 'green' Broad Down, visited more by sheep than walkers. This is a quiet place to retreat and be at peace with your thoughts.

South from the cairn, the high path leads us to 'ghostly' Hangman's Hill (906ft), then Shire Ditch to the distorted trees that guard the southern approach. As the name suggests, there were once gibbets on this hill. The lower path leads us past Giant's Cave, also know as Clutter's Cave. Some think it may have been used by druids, or was home to a hermit. Others believe it is just a Victorian folly. A large flat stone once lay below the cave, believed to have been used as a sacrificial stone; this is now in Colwall. Below Hangman's is the tranquil setting of Pink Cottage overlooking the marshy Castlemarton Common. The junction of paths here is known as Silurian Pass and is the site of

an ancient east–west track. Stand here for a short while, look down the westward track and you can feel the spirits of people past toiling over the pass with donkey's and carts.

From here the hills take on a whole new perspective. No more the hubbub of tourists and casual dog walkers but real history. Ancient trees and track ways much more visible. The western track leads you to the common, dotted with ponds and pollarded black willows.

The next peak is 'sharp' Swinyard Hill (892ft), which takes its name from the time of Edward I. It was granted to the people of Ledbury as upland grazing for their pigs. Swinyard Hill sits between two extremes: to the east, the wide expance of the ancient hunting grounds of Castlemorton Common; to the west, the beautiful, dense, woodland of Eastnor Deer Park.

After ten minutes walking the ridge we discover the final cairn. One arrow points south towards the Gullet, an awesome

Everyone has their own 'best view in Britain'. This happens to be mine.

and infamous Gullet Quarry. The arrow west directs us to Midsummer Hill, the Obelisk and down into the sprawling woodland.

Malvern water has been bottled and sent all over the country and the world from as early as the reign of James I. The rapid growth in popularity of 'the water cure' at Malvern owes much to two doctors: Dr James Wilson and Dr James Manby Gulley. They set up their hydrotherapy centres in Malvern. The water cure consisted of plenty of fresh Malvern water, a great deal of exercise and a strict diet, which may account for its success.

The geology effects the water purity, the Malvern Hills are amongst the oldest and hardest rocks to be found anywhere in the country. The hills sudden rise above the surrounding countryside is a result of action 600 million years ago. During the birth of the hills, the Earth's surface was an altogether different place, the land we now stand on was somewhere south of the equator.

The ancient core of the hills was then being thrust up through the sedimentary rocks that lay above, in a huge earth movement known to geologists as the Cheltenham Drive. Because the core granite rock of the Malverns is extremely hard and the rocks on either side much softer, a phenomenon called 'differential erosion' occurred, where the softer base rocks are worn away by the elements much more quickly than the harder rock. This is what created the distinctive Malverns ridge. At the Gullet Quarry, quarrying work over the years has exposed fine examples of rock strata, which shows how the sedimentary rocks, which were laid down on the seabed horizontally, have been pushed up nearly vertically by the Cheltenham Drive. Geologists from the world over come to the quarry to experience the astonishing rock strata. For the

Far-off Bredon Hill in the Vale of Eversham, like a hippopotamus with its back above the water.

best view of the rock strata, stand at the south side of the flooded quarry, looking north and slightly west at the top of the cliffs. Here you will see the 600 million year old upright rock strata.

From the large deer park gates, head either west for the Obelisk or south for historic Midsummer Hill (932ft), owned by the National Trust. Just past the entrance to a smallholding we peel off left to walk on the original chariot route towards the north gate of the fortress. Rising gently upwards and through a gap in the ramparts, this is where the huge gates would have stood. From here, take the time to look back northwards at the view and the hills already travelled. On the peak of Midsummer Hill the terraced ramparts are clearly visible, more so to the west with extensive views towards Eastnor Castle. Below and to the east is wooded Hollybush Hill, still part of the fortress but less visible beneath the trees. It is interesting to note that this is the only hill with any structure on the top. In the small storm shelter is a plaque stating 'This Iron-Age hill fort was given to the National Trust in 1923 in memory of Captain Reginald Somers-Cocks M.C.'

Continuing south we discover the two huge Hollybush quarries, both with steep sides and very dangerous. One is flooded, the other a rifle range, so the wise stay well away.

Crossing the main Tewkesbury–Ledbury road (with great care), our next peak, or to be correct, two peaks, is 'mystic' Raggedstone Hill (820ft), long associated with druid worship. The steep path runs up the northern side, with fine views to the north and west. This path delivers us to the bare west peak. Stay a while to take in the views, the east peak is easily accessible and worth the short walk.

No tale of the Malverns is better known or more tragic than that of the Monk of Little Malvern Priory; he lapsed in his vow of chastity and confessed his sins. The Prior sentenced him to an awful penance, that he should each day for one year crawl on his hands and knees to the top of Raggedstone Hill. And for many weeks he did, until one day, exhausted and bleeding the deranged young monk rose in despair on the summit and cursed the hill, the prior, the church and all the people upon whom the shadow of the hill should fall. Then, raising his arms like a cross, he fell dead. Some locals claim to have seen what they think is the ghost of the poor monk still climbing on all fours, to the top of the hill.

Looking south towards the gentle rolling landscape is interrupted only by our last objective: Chase End Hill (625ft), 'the guardian of the south'. Descend the steep slopes of Raggedstone Hill to the quiet, tranquil setting that is Whiteleaved Oak, no more than a hamlet, and a forgotten corner of the Malvern Hills. Having wandered the length of the hills along the Herefordshire–Worcestershire county boundary, taking the narrow and sometime muddy footpath to Chase End Hill, we find ourselves in Gloucestershire. This path winds its way through the wooded lower slopes and steepens towards the peak and the trig point. Good views of Raggedstone Hill are to be had but almost all of the other hills are obscured. Sitting upon this hill, enjoy the solitude and absolute deafening silence.

I hope the landscape fires your imagination and you enjoy the 'Spirit of the Hills'.

Mike Smart

Up here on Chase End Hill the silence is deafening.
Sit, look, and let your mind have some time off.

This beautiful, lonely contorted tree stands at the southern end of
Hangman's Hill.

From Sugarloaf Hill looking south towards British Camp.
Just visible on the left is Midsummer Hill.

ABOVE
British Camp, here with a light dusting of snow.
Beyond is May Hill in a sea-like mist.

RIGHT
On Hangman's Hill you'll discover this and other
contorted trees. They stand on the edge the Shire
Ditch like guardians keeping a watchful eye over the
common below.

Warm spring sun brings forth the blossom at this cottage
garden below Raggedstone Hill.

ABOVE
The Seat, a sharp rocky outcrop on the eastern slopes of North Hill, makes a stark contrast to the distant smooth, rounded top of Worcestershire Beacon.

RIGHT
A lightning-struck tree silhouetted against the evening sky below End Hill. Unfortunately the tree is no longer standing as it was brought down by recent high winds.

ABOVE

A cold snap enhances this stunning view from Rookery Rocks below Worcestershire Beacon, looking south towards Summer Hill, Pinnacle Hill and British Camp.

RIGHT

Standing on history. From below this rock outcrop we see Shire Ditch snaking its way along the ridge and southwards into the distance.

All paths lead to the Beacon, or that's how it looks from North Hill.

LEFT
Making the most of the sunshine, above the mist on British
Camp.

ABOVE
The magnificence of Herefordshire Beacon, British Camp
Iron Age hill fort, viewed from Millennium Hill looking north.
Popular folklore has it that the ancient British chieftain
Caractacus made his last stand here against the Romans.

The sharpness of Rookery Rocks contrasts with the soft folds of Pinnacle Hill and British Camp.

LEFT
Not all the spectacular views the Malverns have to offer are to found on or near the ridge. Shortly after a rain shower, nature provides this wonderful light show, on one of the many eastern slope paths.

BELOW
During warm summer days, this quiet path on the western slopes of Worcestershire Beacon offers welcome shade and stunning views in equal portions.

LEFT
Raggedstone Hill, very different from the better known hills to the north and the only hill with two peaks, east and west. Its reputation is mystical and it has associations with sun worship. A number of leys are believed to run through the hill.

BELOW
The traps are set. Sit back, enjoy the view and wait for lunch to turn up.

LEFT
Giant's Cave, Clutter's Cave and Walm's Cave are all names given to this strange hole in the rocks. There are many accounts of how this cave came to be, depending on who you talk to. It is either a hermitage, a druid's cave or a Victorian folly.

LEFT
The rollercoaster ridge path of the northern hills is clearly visible. A hard, but extrmely satisfying day's walking can be accomplished by starting at the clock tower below End Hill at the north end, walking south over every peak to Chase End Hill and returning by the same route. All this in less than seven hours: thirty-three peaks, 6,000 feet of ascent and endless views.

TOP
Morning sun streams through the leafless trees providing this spectral light on the slopes of Midsummer Hill.

ABOVE
Stubborn North Hill basks in the morning sunshine, its appearance softened by this welcome rainbow.

Their beauty revealed to full effect, Perseverance Hill, Pinnacle Hill
and British Camp from Summer Hill.

Midsummer's Day early morning. From Broad Down
at 3.45am, the Malverns look totally serene . . .

. . . . an hour later the same morning, the true splendour of Midsummer's Day is revealed.

43

ABOVE
A chilly morning from below Sugarloaf Hill looking west across Green Valley.

LEFT
An early morning outing on the hills.

ABOVE
Sunshine floods across this carpet of bluebells on the northerns slopes of Raggedstone Hill.

RIGHT
There are supposedly in the region of 100 freshwater springs to be found in the Malvern Hills, some well known and well used for the collection of water; others, like this one, hidden away.

Trees on the western side silhouetted against the evening sky.

Looking through the ferns below End Hill towards the setting sun.

The watery, wintery sun rises behind Raggedstone Hill.

Extremes of light and dark soften the humped-back shape of Bredon Hill.

ABOVE
During a cloud inversion the town and surrounding countryside take on a completely different, fairytale appearance.

RIGHT
In the still of the evening, a hot air balloon rises slowly from the grounds of Eastnor Castle to drift languidly over British Camp.

ABOVE
The rollercoaster ridge path is clearly visible after this dusting of snow.

LEFT
The Obelisk, erected to the Honourable Edward Charles Cocks, eldest son of Lord Somers, dominates the uplands of Eastnor Deer Park, and is seen here pointing directly at the distinctive silhouette of May Hill in the distant Forest of Dean.

Green Valley. The colours are like daubs skillfully applied by an artist's brush.

It is almost a case of 'follow the yellow brick road'. Here we see the Lady Howard de Walden's Path heading south past Sugarloaf Hill and on towards Worcestershire Beacon. Interestingly, from here you can clearly see Shire Ditch, also known as the Red Earl's Ditch, running up from Green Valley and over the Beacon.

From the west side of Sugarloaf Hill, British Camp and the Obelisk. In the far distance May Hill, in the Forest of Dean, floats silently in the mist.

LEFT ABOVE

Views of the hills or from the hills are equally stunning. Looking north-west from Perseverance Hill.

LEFT BELOW

The Malverns may only be seven miles in length and just under 1,400 feet at their highest point, but the spirit is huge and the moods are endless.

BELOW

A solitary tree shown off to full advantage: a green island in a sea of bright yellow rape seed just below Little Malvern.

ABOVE
The sun starts to burn off the morning mist, creating this diagonal striped effect above Holy Well.

RIGHT
A tree with a view. This silver birch, with its outstretched branches, reminds me of an artist or photographer holding up his hands to imagine this view with a picture frame around it.

ABOVE
The southern ramparts of British Camp now known as Millennium Hill bathed in the morning sunshine, with Midsummer Hill just visible beyond.

RIGHT
For some reason, these sheep grazing below North Hill are not interested in this sunrise in the slightest!

ABOVE
The trig pillar on top of
Worcestershire Beacon marks
the highest point on the
range, at 1,395 feet.

RIGHT
With a flask of tea and a great
view, this lone walker sits
looking east on Summer Hill.

Any tree in full summer leaf holds a wonder all of its own.

Sunshine, frost and Worcestershire Beacon from Summer Hill.

Jack Frost nipping at your ears, you just can't beat an early morning walk on the hills.

A summer evening looking north across Green Valley
towards Table Hill and North Hill.

ABOVE
Mistletoe dots this lonely tree on Hangman's Hill.

RIGHT
Above Wyche Cutting looking south. A sharp eye will discover this view of Perseverance Hill, with Shire Ditch visible running along its eastern side.

FAR RIGHT
Shire Ditch, visible here on Pinnacle Hill, looking north over Jubilee Hill towards Worcestershire Beacon.

The sun's rays fan across the Vale of Eversham, providing a spectacular show on a dull frosty day.

Castlemorton Common swathed in mist.

LEFT
Shy Summer Hill, passed and
missed by many on their hasty trek
to the Beacon.

BELOW
A hale storm sweeps across
Herefordshire towards the
Malverns viewed from
Perseverance Hill.

Foxgloves, sunshine and a view of British Camp.

Are you sitting comfortably?

ABOVE
Sheep may safely graze . . . as they do here on Hangman's Hill.

RIGHT
Ghosts on Hangman's Hill?

A lonely tree on the western slopes of the Beacon.

During the cloud inversion, a distant hill, viewed from Jubilee Hill, takes on the form of an island in the cotton wool sea.

RIGHT ABOVE
From the cairn at Dingle top, stubborn old North Hill bathes in the winter sunshine. Its broad shoulders protect the other hills from the cold north winds.

RIGHT BELOW
End Hill. Quiet and unassuming, shyly hiding away from the crowds at the far north end.

This view of the Malvern Hills looking north from British Camp is the most popular and most photographed view of the entire range.

On the hills, there can be fewer places better suited to watching the day blur into evening than here at the top of the Dingle.

RIGHT

Local folklore says that pixies and fairies once dwelt in this peaceful dell below North Hill. But the building of the reservoir above Jubilee Clock Tower in 1880s drove them away forever.

BELOW

Here on Hangman's Hill above Pink Cottage, Shire Ditch is clearly visible striking its way up the hillside.

To some, the Sacred Oak, branches hung with coloured ribbons, trinkets and offerings, is a
very mystical and spiritual place, totally peaceful.

The popularity of the water cure owes much to Dr Wilson and Dr Gulley. The first water cure centre in Great Malvern opened in 1842, clients would have been treated using water from St Ann's Well. The walk from the town by way of the ninety-nine steps then the zigzag path to St Ann's Well is worth the effort. The well and café, set in their quiet sheltered valley, are the ideal place for morning coffee.

One frosty morning on my way up Raggedstone Hill
I encountered this amazing view.

ABOVE
Holy Well. It is said that the healing powers of Malvern water, now famous throughout the world, were first noted in 1622.

LEFT
Foliage decorated pillars at Great Malvern station.

The ninety-nine steps by Rose Bank
Gardens will eventually lead you to
St Ann's Well.

RIGHT
The sunshine striking its way
through the wood above Royal Well.

Little Malvern Court, nestling among the trees and fish ponds, adjacent to Little
Malvern Priory Church. Above are Tinkers Hill and Herefordshire Beacon.

The peaceful Little Malvern Priory Church is all that remains of the twelfth-century Benedictine monastery.

Just one small field benefits from a single shaft of welcome sunlight,
at the start of a very stormy day.

The Obelisk, high above Eastnor Dear Park, is a visible landmark
from almost every peak on the range.

The Beacon toposcope, erected in commemoration of the sixtieth year of Queen Victoria's reign in 1897, is inscribed: 'The Earth is the Lord's and the followers thereof.'

A bench with a view, below Table Hill.

The Beacon over Third's Land.

Almost without detail, the Eastnor Deer Park obelisk pointing
towards May Hill in the Forest of Dean.

ABOVE
Herefordshire Beacon wearing its winter face.

RIGHT
Sunshine highlighting the ridge path and Shire Ditch
running over Black Hill and Perseverance Hill.

FOLLOWING PAGES
What's waiting around the next bend?
In the Malverns you never know.

A magical cloud inversion that lasted all day. Absolute stillness and silence.
Bredon Hill across the vale.

Sheep trails and footpaths strike out across
Herefordshire Beacon like a huge spider's web.

RIGHT
Eastnor Castle, viewed
from the steep climb up
Raggedstone Hill. It is
Norman Revival in style:
not as old as it appears.

BELOW
A peaceful setting: Little
Malvern Priory Church.

LEFT
Is it just me it happens to? Whenever I stop to take a picture of sheep, they turn on their heels and run away, leaving me with yet another shot of retreating sheep!

BELOW
Stooping towards the lush green meadow on Castlemorton Common.

North Hill, in autumn colours.

Looking north along the rollercoaster ridge from Pinnacle Hill. The first peak is Jubilee Hill, named in 2002 in celebration of the Queen's Golden Jubilee. Then, Perseverance Hill leading to Wyche Cutting and then Summer Hill, blending into the lower slopes of Worcestershire Beacon.

LEFT
How many times have we wished we could have been the first
to leave footprints in the pure white snow?

ABOVE
No chance of being the first here. The slate-grey sky looms
menacingly over the hills with more snow to come. Looking
north from British Camp.

A rather spooky landscape, looking over Swinyard Hill with
Midsummer Hill beyond.

A bird's-eye view of the common at Link Top from North Hill.

LEFT
Some folk believe woodland spirits live in the trees. In the dark, leafless season of winter, the spirits take refuge in the holly tree.

TOP
British Camp, constructed in the fourth century BC and altered over the centuries that followed. It's easy to understand why Elgar was so inspired by this giant hill.

ABOVE
One relaxing and inspirational view just keeps leading you on to another.

LEFT
Great Malvern Priory started life as a Benedictine monastey
in c.1075. During the reign of Edward the Confessor, the
Bishop of Worcester, encouraged a hermit, Aldwyn, to found
a monastery in what was then the wooded wilderness of
Malvern Chase.

ABOVE
The Priory looms over the ivy-covered Abbey Hotel, in the
centre of Great Malvern.

'Pretty in pink', as the saying goes.

British Camp framed to perfection by this ancient oak on Black Hill.

OVERLEAF
'It is the journey and not the arriving that excites us.' Our journey here is nearly done.

INDEX